GABRIELA POPA

Coloring Patterns
An Inspiring Coloring Book Featuring Relaxing Shapes, Flowers and Animals

Pixiphoria

Published in 2015 by
Pixiphoria
St. Louis, MO

Copyright © 2015 Gabriela Popa

ISBN-13: 978-0-9838641-5-8

Designed and printed in the United States of America

From the library of

_____

Date _____

Location _____

Author _____

Date

Location

Author

Date _____

Location _____

Author _____

Date _____

Location _____

Author _____

Date _____

Location _____

Author _____

Date _____

Location _____

Author _____

Date

Location

Author

Date _____

Location _____

Author _____

Date

Location

Author

Date _____

Location _____

Author _____

Date _____

Location _____

Author _____

Date _____

Location _____

Author _____

Date _____

Location _____

Author _____

Date

Location

Author

Date _____

Location _____

Author _____

Date _____

Location _____

Author _____

Date _____

Location _____

Author _____

Date

Location

Author

Date

Location

Author

Date _____

Location _____

Author _____

Date _____

Location _____

Author _____

Date _____

Location _____

Author _____

Date _____

Location _____

Author _____

Date _____

Location _____

Author _____

Date _____

Location _____

Author _____

Date _____

Location _____

Author _____

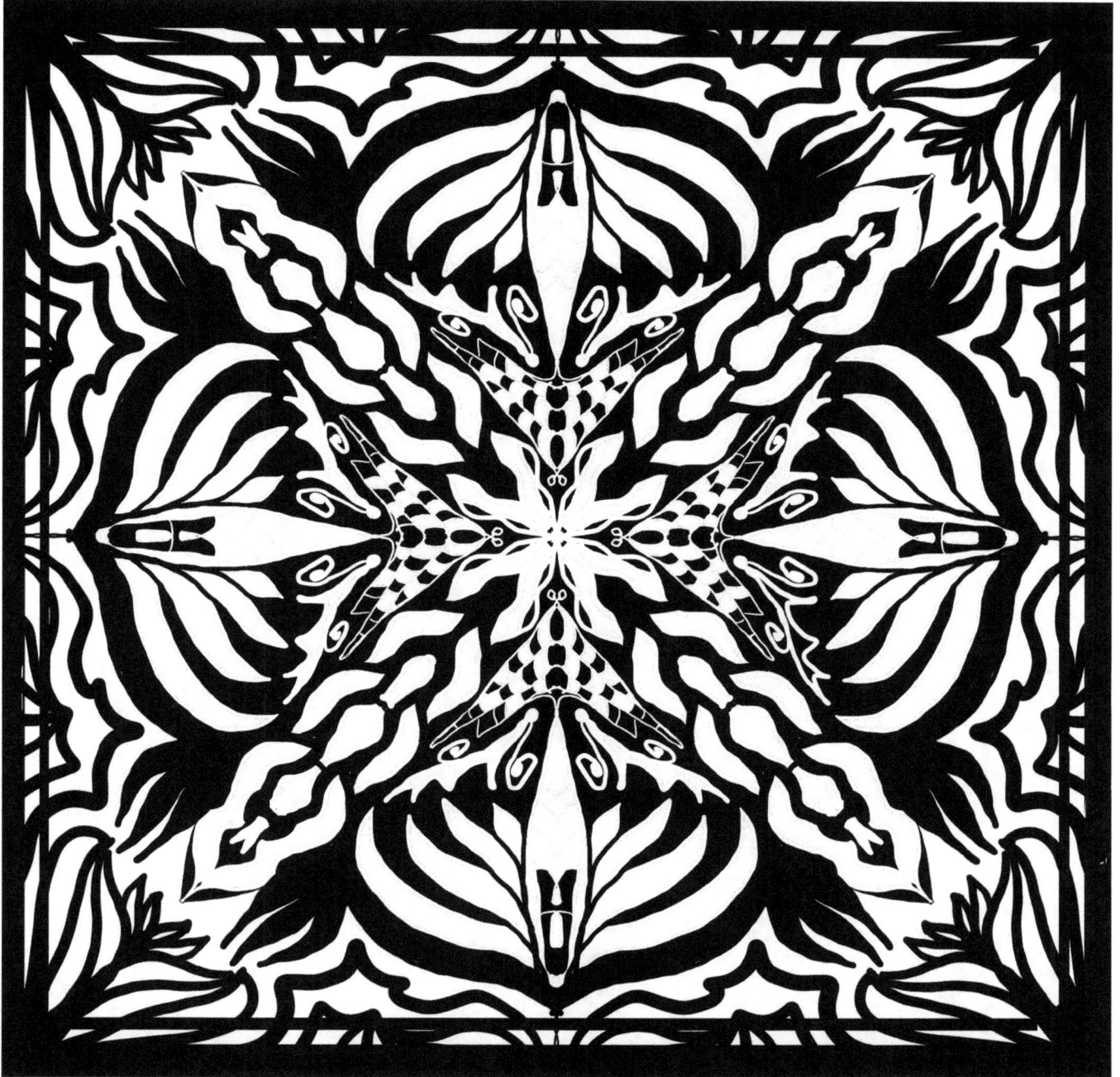

Date _____

Location _____

Author _____

Date _____

Location _____

Author _____

Date

Location

Author

Date _____

Location _____

Author _____

Date _____

Location _____

Author _____

Date _____

Location _____

Author _____

Date _____

Location _____

Author _____

Date _____

Location _____

Author _____

Date _____

Location _____

Author _____

Date _____

Location _____

Author _____

Date _____

Location _____

Author _____

Date _____

Location _____

Author _____

Date

Location

Author

Date

Location

Author

Date _____

Location _____

Author _____

Date _____

Location _____

Author _____

Date _____

Location _____

Author _____

Date

Location

Author

Also by Gabriela Popa:

■ *Focus Your Mind*
(coloring book)
■ **Stressful Day, Melt Away!**
(coloring book)
■ *Kafka's House*
(novel)
■ **When the Moon Had Feet** &
Dragonfly
(stories)

Available in bookstores
including amazon.com

www.ingramcontent.com/pod-product-compliance
Lightning Source LLC
LaVergne TN
LVHW080042090426
835510LV00042B/1933